Old Testament
Adventures

A PLAY & LEARN BOOK

Edited by Jill C. Lafferty
Illustrations by Peter Grosshauser

SPARK
HOUSE
FAMILY

Old Testament Adventures

Epic floods and frogs falling from the sky! Battles with giants and men being swallowed by fish! Bold queens and brave prophets standing up for God! The Old Testament is filled with stories of God's people experiencing all kinds of wild, weird, even scary adventures.

Life with God is a big adventure, and while you probably won't ever fight a giant with a slingshot, you will have times when you need to be brave or be kind to someone who hasn't been kind to you. You might have to be like Daniel and make a choice about listening to God. You might have to be like Esther and trust that God is with you in a hard situation. You might have to be like Joseph and forgive someone who's hurt you.

This Play and Learn book is filled with stories that show us what it looks like to follow God, no matter what. Some of the people in these stories make good decisions, but a few ignore God and do their own thing instead. But in every story, we find God guiding, protecting, and loving God's people, helping them get through every challenge they face.

As you and your family explore these stories from the Old Testament, see if you can find a story where someone:

- Stands up for what they know is right
- Follows God even when they face real danger for doing so
- Shows love and care for others

Each story in this Play and Learn book gives you a verse to remember, some fun activities to try, and ideas for living the way Jesus taught us to. So jump in and discover more about these Old Testament Adventures!

Published by Sparkhouse Family
510 Marquette Avenue
Minneapolis, MN 55402
sparkhouse.org

© 2016 Sparkhouse Family

All rights reserved.

Old Testament Adventures
Play and Learn Book
First edition published 2016

Printed in United States
21 20 19 18 17 16   1 2 3 4 5 6 7 8
9781506417653

Edited by Jill C. Lafferty
Cover design by Tory Herman
Cover illustration by Peter Grosshauser
Interior designed by Tory Herman
Interior photographs provided by
iStock and Thinkstock
Illustrations by Peter Grosshauser

All Bible quotations are from THE HOLY BIBLE, NEW INTERNATIONAL VERSION®, NIV®. Copyright © 1973, 1978, 1984, 2011 by Biblica, Inc.® Used by permission of Zondervan. All rights reserved worldwide. www.zondervan.com. The "NIV" and "New International Version" are trademarks registered in the United States Patent and Trademark Office by Biblica, Inc.™

V63474; 9781506417646; JUN2016

Table of Contents

How to Use Your Spark Story Bible Play and Learn Book

Each section in this Play and Learn book includes a short story from the Bible, followed by all kinds of engaging ways to think about the theme of the story. Look for these activities in every story.

A Prayer to Share
Cut out these prayers to help you talk to God about what you've learned.

ON dark stormy days,
and bright clear nights,
during silent snowstorms,
or crashing thunder,
we remember your
promise, O God. Amen.

Noah's Ark

Let's remember God's promise.

Two aardvarks, two llamas, two ostriches! Noah herded the animals onto the ark. Outside, it rained for 40 days and nights. Inside, Noah and his family cared for every kind of living thing. When the waters went down, the animals left the ark. God spread a rainbow across the sky as a promise to never flood the whole earth again.

When will it stop raining?
How does YOUR face look when you feel restless?

WHAT WOULD YOU PACK FOR A TRIP?
WHO TAKES CARE OF YOU?

The Story
Start here. You'll get a summary of the Bible story you'll explore on the pages to come.

Conversation Starters
Talk about these questions as a family. Make sure everyone gets a chance to share their thoughts.

Explore with Squiggles
This expressive little caterpillar responds to each story with a specific emotion and invites children to do the same.

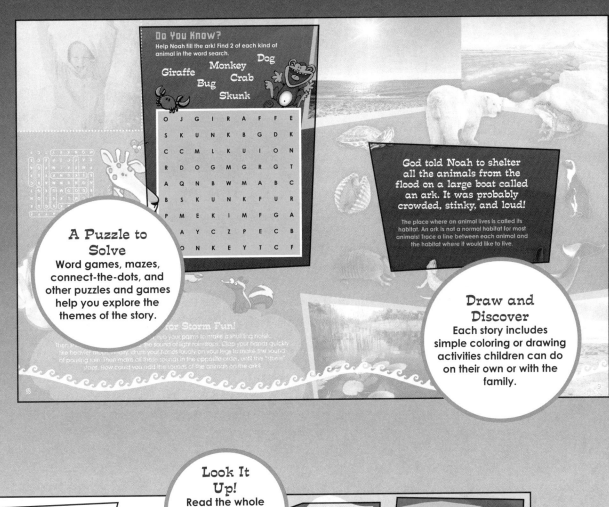

Do You Know?
Help Noah fill the ark! Find 2 of each kind of animal in the word search.

Giraffe Monkey Dog
Bug Crab
Skunk

O	J	G	I	R	A	F	F	E
S	K	U	N	K	B	G	D	K
C	C	M	L	K	U	I	O	N
R	D	O	G	M	G	R	G	T
A	Q	N	B	W	M	A	B	C
B	S	K	U	N	K	F	U	R
P	M	E	K	I	M	F	G	A
A	Y	C	Z	P	E	C	B	S
M	O	N	K	E	Y	T	C	F

A Puzzle to Solve
Word games, mazes, connect-the-dots, and other puzzles and games help you explore the themes of the story.

God told Noah to shelter all the animals from the flood on a large boat called an ark. It was probably crowded, stinky, and loud!

The place where an animal lives is called its habitat. An ark is not a normal habitat for most animals! Trace a line between each animal and the habitat where it would like to live.

Draw and Discover
Each story includes simple coloring or drawing activities children can do on their own or with the family.

Look It Up!
Read the whole story for yourselves from your Bible or *Spark Story Bible*.

In the Bible AND In Our World!
Millions of species of animals live on the earth. This includes more than:
36 kinds of felines (members of the cat family)
9,000 kinds of birds
4,740 kinds of frogs

Insects are harder to count, but some scientists estimate there could be **30,000,000** kinds of bugs!

Can you imagine them all on the ark? How do you think Noah arranged them?

...MORE to this story!
...WHOLE story in your Bible together!
...can find it in the book before Exodus:
Genesis 6–9
In the Spark Story Bible, look for Noah's Ark on pages 24-29.

I have set my rainbow in the clouds, and it will be the sign of the covenant between me and the earth.
Genesis 9:13

Find scarves, T-shirts, hats, or socks in the colors of the rainbow.

While one family member reads this verse out loud, wave the colors in the air. Can you find any rainbow designs around your home that remind you of God's promise?

In Our World
Find out more about how the themes of the stories show up in our lives today.

A Verse to Learn
Say these verses together or try to memorize them as a family.

Make Time for Tent Fun!
The next time there is bad weather outside, build a tent indoors out of blankets and chairs. Can you fit your whole family in your tent? If you have a pet, bring it along. What is fun about hiding in your tent? How... would you want to stay here?

Family Fun!
Put your learning into action with these family activity ideas.

Noah's Ark

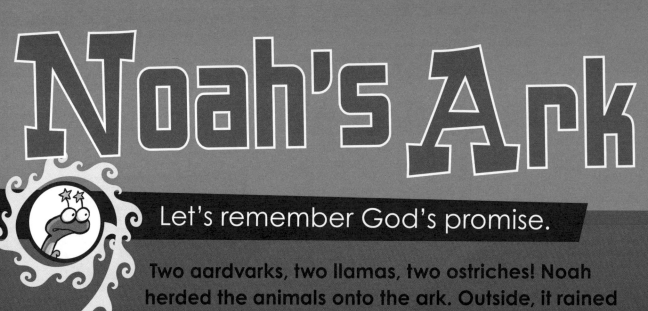

Let's remember God's promise.

Two aardvarks, two llamas, two ostriches! Noah herded the animals onto the ark. Outside, it rained for 40 days and nights. Inside, Noah and his family cared for every kind of living thing. When the waters went down, the animals left the ark. **God spread a rainbow across the sky as a promise to never flood the whole earth again.**

Squiggles feels restless. When will it stop raining? How does YOUR face look when you feel restless?

Cut out this prayer and put it in a coat pocket. When you need to wear the coat because of bad weather, say the prayer together.

ON dark stormy days, and bright clear nights, during silent snowstorms, or crashing thunder, we remember your promise, O God. Amen.

WHAT WOULD YOU PACK FOR A TRIP?
WHO TAKES CARE OF YOU?

Do You Know?

Help Noah fill the ark! Find 2 of each kind of animal in the word search.

Giraffe　**Monkey**　**Dog**
Bug　**Crab**
Skunk

O	J	G	I	R	A	F	F	E
S	K	U	N	K	B	G	D	K
C	C	M	L	K	U	I	O	N
R	D	O	G	M	G	R	G	T
A	Q	N	B	W	M	A	B	C
B	S	K	U	N	K	F	U	R
P	M	E	K	I	M	F	G	A
E	A	Y	C	Z	P	E	C	B
M	O	N	K	E	Y	T	C	F

Make Time for Storm Fun!

Act out a storm together. First, rub your palms to make a shuffling noise. Then snap your fingers to make the sound of light raindrops. Clap your hands quickly like heavier drops. Finally, drum your hands loudly on your legs to make the sound of pouring rain. Then make all these sounds in the opposite order, until the "storm" stops. How could you add the sounds of the animals on the ark?

God told Noah to shelter all the animals from the flood on a large boat called an ark. It was probably crowded, stinky, and loud!

The place where an animal lives is called its habitat. An ark is not a normal habitat for most animals! Trace a line between each animal and the habitat where it would like to live.

In the Bible AND In Our World!

Millions of species of animals live on the earth. This includes more than:

36 kinds of felines (members of the cat family)
9,000 kinds of birds
4,740 kinds of frogs

Insects are harder to count, but some scientists estimate there could be
30,000,000 kinds of bugs!

Can you imagine them all on the ark?
How do you think Noah arranged them?

Make Time for Tent Fun!

The next time there is bad weather outside, build a tent indoors out of blankets and chairs. Can you fit your whole family in your tent? If you have a pet, bring it along too! What is fun about hiding in your tent? How long would you want to stay here?

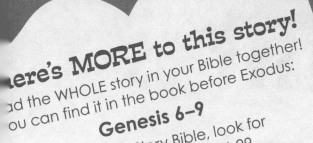

There's MORE to this story!

Read the WHOLE story in your Bible together! You can find it in the book before Exodus:

Genesis 6–9

In the Spark Story Bible, look for Noah's Ark on pages 24-29.

I have set my **rainbow in the clouds,** and it will be the sign of the covenant between me and the earth.

Genesis 9:13

Find scarves, T-shirts, hats, or socks in the colors of the rainbow.

While one family member reads this verse out loud, wave the colors in the air. Can you find any rainbow designs around your home that remind you of God's promise?

Red

Yellow

Orange

Blue

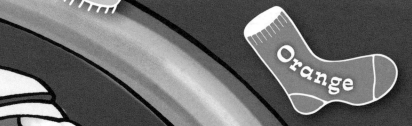

Green

Indigo

Violet

Rebekah and Isaac

God's promises keep growing.

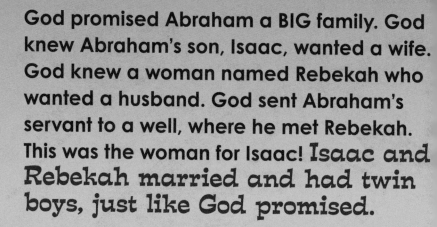

God promised Abraham a BIG family. God knew Abraham's son, Isaac, wanted a wife. God knew a woman named Rebekah who wanted a husband. God sent Abraham's servant to a well, where he met Rebekah. This was the woman for Isaac! Isaac and Rebekah married and had twin boys, just like God promised.

Squiggles feels hopeful. God's family is growing.

How does YOUR face look when you feel hopeful?

Cut out this prayer, tape it to a doll or stuffed toy, and cradle the toy as you say the prayer together.

DEAR GOD, thank you for keeping your promise to Rebekah and Isaac, and thank you for all babies! Amen.

WHO IS IN YOUR FAMILY? WHAT'S HARD ABOUT GETTING ALONG WITH FAMILY MEMBERS?

God changed Abram's name to Abraham to show that God remembered the promise!

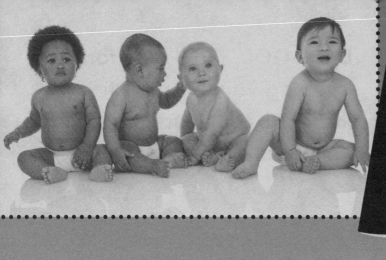

There's MORE to this stor

Read the WHOLE story in your Bible toget
You can find it in the 1st Old Testament bo

Genesis 24; 25:19-28

In the Spark Story Bible, look for
Rebekah and Isaac on pages 42-45.

God led Abraham's servant to a well, where Rebekah gave him and his camels water.

In Bible times, a well was a central meeting place, especially for women. Today, friends and family gather around water for lots of different activities. Have you ever done any of these things?

Draw your favorite thing to do in or around water with family and friends.

raham was now very old,
nd the LORD had blessed
him in every way.

Genesis 24:1

ay this verse together, and take turns
haming ways God has blessed your
nily. Write those blessings below. After
you name something, say together,
The Lord has blessed us!"

God has blessed our family!

Do You Know?

Rebekah and Isaac's twins, Jacob and Esau,
looked VERY different and acted VERY different.
Read Genesis 25:25-27 to help you fill in the blanks
about Jacob and Esau.

heel   red   home   hairy   hand   hunter

1. The first to come out was _____ _____ _____ , and

his whole body was like a _____ _____ _____ _____

garment; so they named him Esau.

2. After this, his brother came out, with his

_____ _____ _____ _____ grasping Esau's

_____ _____ _____ _____ ; so he was named

Jacob.

3. Esau was a skillful

_____ _____ _____ _____ _____ _____ .

4. Jacob was content to stay

_____ _____ _____ _____ .

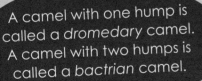

A camel with one hump is
called a *dromedary* camel.
A camel with two humps is
called a *bactrian* camel.

Make Time for More Fun!

Pretend to be a camel like the ones in this
story! Ask someone at home to tie a pillow
on your back. Get down on your hands and
knees and pretend you are traveling with
Abraham's servant to find Rebekah.

How far will you travel?   Where will you get water?

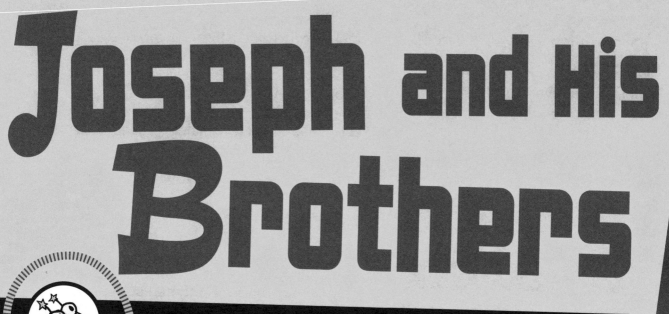

Joseph and His Brothers

Sometimes families don't get along.

Joseph's older brothers were really mad at him. Their father had given Joseph a special coat. They didn't get new coats. Joseph had dreams that made him think he was better than his brothers. The brothers had heard enough! They became even more angry and sad, and their father, Jacob, was mad at Joseph too.

Cut out this prayer and use it as a bookmark in your family Bible or Spark Story Bible. Say the prayer when family members are angry with each other.

DEAR GOD, sometimes we get angry with the people in our family. Help us to love each other. Amen.

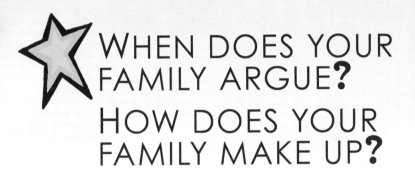

WHEN DOES YOUR FAMILY ARGUE? HOW DOES YOUR FAMILY MAKE UP?

Squiggles feels mad. Everyone's angry! How does YOUR face look when you feel mad?

Families do more than argue.

They play together, work together, eat together, and more. Look at the photos. Do you do some of these things with your family? Make a list of things your family does together.

Things we do together:

There's MORE to this story!

Read the WHOLE story in your Bible together! You can find it in the 1st book of the Old Testament:

Genesis 37:1-28

In the Spark Story Bible, look for Joseph and His Brothers on pages 50-55.

Do You Know?

Families in the Bible didn't get along all of the time. Find these stories to help you fill in the blanks and learn about Bible family fights.

1. _____ and _____ fought even before they were born! (See Genesis 25:21-26.)

2. _____'s brother Eliab scolded him. (See 1 Samuel 17:28-30.)

3. _____ was angry when her sister, _____, didn't help with the housework. (See Luke 10:38-42.)

> When his brothers saw that their father loved him more than any of them, they hated him, and could not speak a kind word to him.
> Genesis 37:4

What are things you can do when it's hard to speak calmly with each other? Say the verse together, and then practice things that your family can do when words are hard: **take a deep breath, give a hug, hold a hand. Do you have other ideas?**

Make Time for More Fun!

Take a silly family photo. Together, think of some silly poses for a family photograph. You could wear costumes, have wild hair-dos, make funny faces, or anything that will make you laugh. Print the funniest photo and put it on your refrigerator. In times when family members are unhappy with each other, look at the photo to remember why you love each other.

The Burning Bush

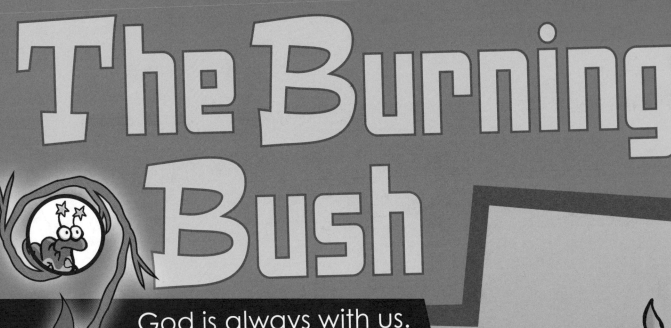

God is always with us.

Moses was tending his sheep when he saw a bush on fire! A talking bush, no less. God appeared to Moses in the bush to ask him to lead God's people out of Egypt. Moses would have to confront Pharaoh, the leader of Egypt! Moses was nervous, but God would be with him.

HOW WOULD YOU LIKE TO HEAR GOD?

HOW WOULD YOU ANSWER GOD?

GOD, thank you for always being with us. Amen.

Squiggles feels terrified. The bush is talking! How does YOUR face look when you feel terrified?

Cut out this prayer and tape it to a mirror. Look in the mirror and say the prayer together, remembering that God is always right there beside you!

There's MORE to this story

Read the WHOLE story in your Bible togethe
You can find it in the 2nd book in the Bible

Exodus 3:1-15

In the Spark Story Bible, look for the Old
Testament story The Burning Bush on pages 7

God asked Moses to do something hard! What hard things do you do?

Look at the photos. Circle the photo that you think is the most difficult. Cross out the scariest. Draw a smiley face near the one that would be most fun! No matter what you do, God is with you.

"Do not come any closer," God said. "Take off your sandals, for the place where you are standing is holy ground."

Exodus 3:5

Take turns reading this verse to each other. When you are the reader, point to another person before you begin reading. That person has to take off their shoes when God tells Moses to do so!

In the Bible AND In Our World!

God appearing in fire was sure to catch Moses' attention! Today, fire brings us together—we light candles at church and enjoy gathering around a campfire. But fire can be scary and destructive when it's out of control. What a great image of God's power and mystery!

Make Time for More Fun!

God told Moses that he was standing on holy ground. Where are the holy places in your life—the places where you honor and feel closest to God? Together with your family, make a list of places (not just church!) that are holy ground to you. If you can, go to some of these places and take pictures to create a "holy ground" collage. If you can't go to some of them, draw pictures of those places.

The Plagues

God gave Moses a big message for Pharaoh: Let the Hebrew people go! But Pharaoh wouldn't listen. So God sent 10 plagues to get Pharaoh's attention. Frogs, gnats, flies, and locusts swarmed the land! One frog is small, but thousands crowded Pharaoh's palace. One locust is tiny, but a cloud of them devoured Egypt's crops. Pharaoh couldn't ignore God's message any longer!

WHO LISTENS TO YOU?
WHEN HAVE YOU DONE A BIG JOB?

Squiggles feels surprised. Where did all these frogs come from? How does YOUR face look when you feel surprised?

A plague is a widespread disease or natural disaster.

Cut out this prayer along the dotted lines and then cut out each section. Now you have 9 little prayers! Hide them around your house so that your family can see and say them wherever they go. Once they've been found, gather all the prayers together. Turn them over and see if you can put the puzzle together.

Thanks, God, for doing big things! Amen.	Thanks, God, for doing big things! Amen.	Thanks, God, for doing big things! Amen.
Thanks, God, for doing big things! Amen.	Thanks, God, for doing big things! Amen.	Thanks, God, for doing big things! Amen.
Thanks, God, for doing big things! Amen.	Thanks, God, for doing big things! Amen.	Thanks, God, for doing big things! Amen.

God used tiny critters to send a big message.

Follow the paths to see how tiny things are a big part of God's creation.

There's MORE to this story!

Read the WHOLE story in your Bible together!
You can find it in the 2nd book in the Old Testamen

Exodus 7:14—12:32

In the Spark Story Bible, look for
The Plagues on pages 80-85.

Make Time for More Fun!

Put a penny in a jar. The next day, put in two pennies. On the third day, put in three pennies; on the fourth put in four. Continue adding each day. How many days can you keep adding to the jar? When the jar is full, take it to a bank or coin exchange machine and convert the pennies to cash. As a family, decide on a charity and donate the money. Your little pennies can make a big difference!

By this you will know that I am the LORD.

Exodus 7:17

God sent big signs to Pharaoh!

Write each of the words of this verse in big letters on separate sheets of paper. Divide the words among family members. Say the verse together, each person saying their word or words and holding up their sheets of paper. Where could you display this big message in your home?

Do You Know?

God sent 10 plagues to get Pharaoh to listen to Moses. After each plague, Moses repeated the message from God.

Put these words in order to discover Moses' message *(see Exodus 8:1):*

GO   MY   PEOPLE   LET

_____ _____

_____ _____ !

The Red Sea

God helps us be brave!

As Pharaoh's chariots charged closer, the Israelites got frightened.

"Stand firm," Moses said. "God is with us." Then Moses lifted up his staff. The sea parted—

and the people escaped to freedom!

Cut out this prayer, roll it the long way with the words showing, and tape it to make a "staff." Pass it to each family member as you say the prayer together.

WHAT SCARES YOU?
WHEN HAVE YOU BEEN BRAVE?

Squiggles feels joyful!

They're safe from Pharaoh's army! How does **YOUR** face look when you feel joyful?

LEAD us forward, God. Help us to bravely follow you! Amen.

It takes courage to learn how to do new things.

Check off those things that you can do already. God helps us be brave as we keep learning our whole lives!

There's MORE to this story!

Read the WHOLE story in your Bible together! You can find it in the 2nd book of the Old Testament:

Exodus 14:1-30

In the Spark Story Bible, look for *The Red Sea* on pages 86-91.

Make Time for More Fun!

Moses and the Israelites camped on the shore of the Red Sea. In honor of them, pitch a tent and spend a night outdoors! Do some stargazing and cooking over a fire. If there is water nearby, try your hand at fishing or swimming, just like the ancient Israelites might have done.

Do You Know?

Moses and Jesus have something in common. Both were saved from cruel leaders— while they were still babies! Read Exodus 2:1-10 and Matthew 2:13-23 in your Bible to help fill in the blanks.

_____ was saved when his parents took him to Egypt, far away from King Herod.

_____ was saved when his mother put him in a basket on the Nile River to hide him from the King of Egypt.

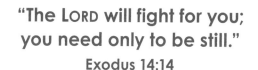

"The LORD will fight for you; you need only to be still."
Exodus 14:14

Find a special spot in your home where you can pray. Write this verse on a blank card, and place it there. Whenever you feel worried or upset, sit in your spot and pray. Remember God is working to help you—even while you're sitting still!

Do You Know? Answers: 1. Jesus, 2. Moses.

31

The Ten Commandments

Let's live together in peace!

The Israelites saw lightning and smoke. They heard thunder and a trumpet! God's voice called Moses to the top of Mount Sinai. When Moses reached the top, God gave him rules for the Israelites. God knew the Israelites needed help on their long journey. The rules helped the Israelites live together in peace. **We call these rules the Ten Commandments!**

Sinai is pronounce **SIGH-nigh.**

WHAT RULES DO YOU FOLLOW?

WHICH RULES HELP MAKE PEACE?

Cut out this prayer and tape it to the inside of your front door. Say it together every time you travel away from home and when you return.

GOD, help us live together in peace at home and on the road! Amen.

quiggles feels orried. He ants Moses be safe.

How does YOUR face look when you feel worried?

Showing love for God and love for others is a way of following God's rules.

Write a **G** on photos that show love for God.

Write an **O** on photos that show love for others.

Do any of the photos show both?

Make Time for Snacking Fun!

Make some traveling food to help keep your tummies peaceful when you are away from home.

CEREAL TRAIL MIX

Mix 1½ cups of your favorite healthy cereal with 1 teaspoon of cinnamon. Add 4 tablespoons of dried fruit and mix. Put trail mix in a food storage container and take it with you on your next trip.

There's MORE to this story!

Read the WHOLE story in your Bible together! You can find it in the 2nd book of the Old Testament:

Exodus 20:1-17

In the Spark Story Bible, look for *The Ten Commandments* on pages 96-101.

You shall have no other gods before me.

Exodus 20:3

Stand up tall on tippy toes and reach for the sky, like a mountain. Make your voice rumble like thunder or blare like a trumpet. Make your arms fly like lightning. Then say this verse together with a big voice. Say it again with a medium voice as your lightning lessens. Say it one more time, in the quietest voice you have, as your arms **make a rainbow.**

In the Bible AND In Our World!

The Israelites were traveling from Egypt to the land where God promised they would be safe and happy. People today who study their journey think their route went through different ancient kingdoms. Mount Sinai is in the country of Egypt on the Sinai Peninsula. Trace the Israelites' journey with your finger. Stop at Mount Sinai to read together God's rules for living in peace!

Honor God above all others.

Do not make idols. There are no other gods for you, only me.

Keep God's name special.

Make the Sabbath special.

Love and respect parents and caregivers.

Don't hurt others with your words or actions.

Be loyal to your husband or wife.

Don't take things that aren't yours.

Tell the truth.

Be happy with what you have.

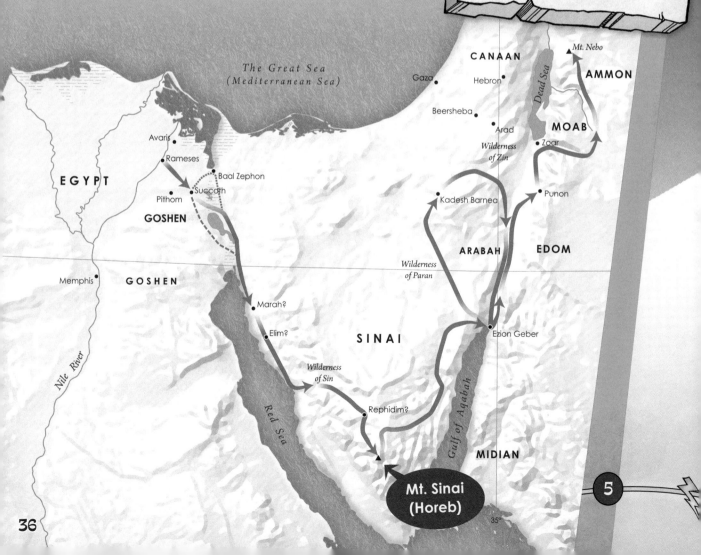

Make Time for Play Clay Fun!

Make a big tablet out of play clay. Pick a commandment you want to remember. Use a toothpick or pencil to carve the commandment into the play clay tablet. Let the tablet dry. Display the tablet on a shelf to help you remember one of God's rules for living together in peace.

What does this word mean to you?

IDOL

COLOR THIS WORD. *Idols* are things that take our time, energy, and talent away from God. One of God's commandments to Moses says that we should focus on God and not on an idol.

The Battle of Jericho

Let's make noise for God!

The Israelites arrived at the land God promised, but tall walls protecting the city of Jericho stood in their way. Joshua led the Israelites in following God's plan: They marched around the city for 6 days. Priests blew loud ram's horn trumpets called shofars, but the other marchers were quiet. On the 7th day, they marched around the city 7 times, then the marchers shouted. SHAKE. CRUMBLE. CRASH. **God brought the walls tumbling down!**

Shofar is pronounc **SHOW-fa**

Squiggles feels joyful. God kept God's promise.

How does **YOUR** face look when yo feel joyful?

Cut out this prayer and role it up into a horn like a shofar. Shout the prayer through it as loud as you can.

MIGHTY GOD, you do great things! We shout our praise to you! Amen.

WHEN HAVE YOU SEEN PEOPLE MARCHING?

HOW DO YOU PRAISE GOD?

surrounded by **thick, strong walls to** protect it.

The city of Jericho was

Look at the walls in these photos. Circle the walls you could knock down. Put a ✓ on the walls God could knock down.

There's MORE to this story!

Read the WHOLE story in your Bible together! You can find it in the 1st historical book in the Old Testament:

Joshua 6:1-20

In the Spark Story Bible, look for *The Battle of Jericho* on pages 102-105.

40

Do You Know? Answers: 1. 7th; 2. 40; 3. 40

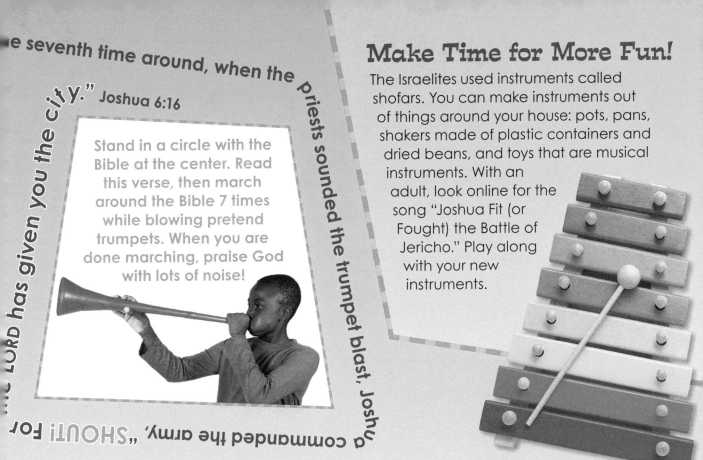

"...seventh time around, when the priests sounded the trumpet blast, Joshua commanded the army, "SHOUT! For the LORD has given you the city." Joshua 6:16

Stand in a circle with the Bible at the center. Read this verse, then march around the Bible 7 times while blowing pretend trumpets. When you are done marching, praise God with lots of noise!

Make Time for More Fun!

The Israelites used instruments called shofars. You can make instruments out of things around your house: pots, pans, shakers made of plastic containers and dried beans, and toys that are musical instruments. With an adult, look online for the song "Joshua Fit (or Fought) the Battle of Jericho." Play along with your new instruments.

Do You Know?

The Israelites marched around the city of Jericho for **7** days, with **7** priests blowing horns. On the **7**th day, they marched around Jericho **7** times. Then the walls came down!

The number **7** is important in the Bible. Here are some other stories that feature numbers. Do you know what number is important in each story?

1. Creation (Genesis 1:1—2:4)
God rested on the _____ day.

2. Noah's Ark (Genesis 6—9)
After Noah's family and the animals were on the ark, it rained for _____ days and nights.

3. Tempted (Luke 4:1-13)
After Jesus was baptized, the Holy Spirit led Jesus into the wilderness, where the devil tempted him for _____ days.

Deborah

God hears and helps!

The Israelites had been captured by their enemies! They prayed for help, and God responded by sending a woman named Deborah, who was a wise and faithful judge. "If you will trust God," Deborah said, "you can defeat your enemies." The Israelites listened to Deborah's message—and God helped them win their freedom!

Squiggles feels scared. How can the Israelites defeat such powerful enemies?

How does YOUR face look when you feel scared?

Cut out this prayer and put it in an envelope. At bedtime, say it together, then slip the envelope under a different family member's pillow each night.

THANK YOU, God, for all you do:
Listening, helping—guiding too!
Watch over those I love tonight,
And keep us safe 'til morning light.
Amen.

WHEN HAVE YOU PRAYED TO GOD?

HOW HAS GOD HELPED YOU?

When the Israelites were captured, God heard their prayers and sent Deborah to help them. God brings helpers into our lives, too. The people in these pictures help others every day. Unscramble the words and write what each person does.

GDEJU

_____

EIFRGRIHFE

_____

AOCHC

_____

EATRCHE

_____

NRUES

_____

Make Time for More Fun!

After being captured by enemies, the Israelites fought to win their freedom. Remind yourselves of their story with the game *Capture the Flag!* Look on the Internet or in a game book for rules, and invite some friends to join you. Celebrate afterward with fruit, cheese, crackers, and juice.

In the Bible AND In Our World!

Today, women hold lots of different jobs. Women are doctors, police officers, pastors, and judges. In Deborah's time, however, this was unusual. In fact, Deborah is the only female judge mentioned in the Bible!

*Barak is pronounced **BEAR-ack**.*

Then Deborah said to Barak, "**Go!** This is the day the LORD has given Sisera into your hands. Has not the LORD gone ahead of you?"
Judges 4:14

Take turns reading the verse while everyone stands. On the word "*go*", everyone starts walking. Stop as soon as you hear "*Has not the Lord gone ahead of you?*" Who got the farthest?

There's MORE to this story!

Read the WHOLE story in your Bible together! You can find it in the 7th book of the Bible:

Judges 4:1—5:31

In the Spark Story Bible, look for *Deborah* on pages 106-109.

HEARS · GOD HELPS · GOD HEARS · GOD HELPS · GOD HEARS · GOD HELPS · GOD HEARS · GOD HELPS · GOD HEARS · GOD HELPS · GOD HEARS · GOD HELPS · GOD

45

Naomi and Ruth

Families do things together!

Naomi and her daughters-in-law, Ruth and Orpah, were running out of food. "You should go live with your mothers," Naomi told them. Orpah sadly returned to her family. But Ruth stayed with Naomi. Together they walked to Naomi's family. Ruth loved Naomi very much, just like God loves each of us!

Squiggles feels loved in Naomi's family. How does YOUR face look when you feel loved?

WHERE DOES YOUR FAMILY LIKE TO GO TOGETHER?

HOW DO YOU WELCOME EACH OTHER HOME?

LOVING GOD, thank you for my family! Please watch over us and bring us home safely. Amen.

Cut out this prayer and carry it in a pocket. Read the prayer when you are apart from your family. Give it to another family member to carry the next day.

Ruth and Naomi loved and cared for each other.

It's fun to work and play with family. Look at the photos. What does your family like to do together? Draw your favorite thing you do as a family in the space below.

In the Bible AND In Our World!

People in Bible times usually had to walk everywhere. They did not have cars or paved roads. Sometimes they could ride animals. Naomi and Ruth walked about 30 miles from Moab to Naomi's home, Bethlehem. Because of the difficult path, it may have taken them seven days to walk that distance. Driving 30 miles today usually takes 30–60 minutes, depending on traffic.

There's MORE to this story!

Read the WHOLE story in your Bible together!
You can find it in the book after Judges:

Ruth 1:1-22

In the Spark Story Bible, look for the Old Testament story titled Naomi and Ruth.

But Ruth said, "Do not press me to leave you or to turn back from following you!
Where you go, I will go; where you lodge, I will lodge; your people shall be my people and your God my God."

Ruth 1:16

Lodge means to spend the night or sleep in a specific place.

With friends or family members, use play dough to make 2 footprints, 2 house shapes, 2 people shapes, and 2 crosses. Read the Bible verse together. Each time you say the **green** words, place the play dough pieces together that match the words.

Make Time for Map Fun!

Imagine a trip you would like to take with your family! Pick a place near or far. Imagine what you might see and do, where you might stay, and what you might eat. With an adult, use a map app or a globe to find directions to the place. How long would it take to get there?

Do You Know? Answers: 1. Quail; 2. Barley; 3. Fish; 4. Bread

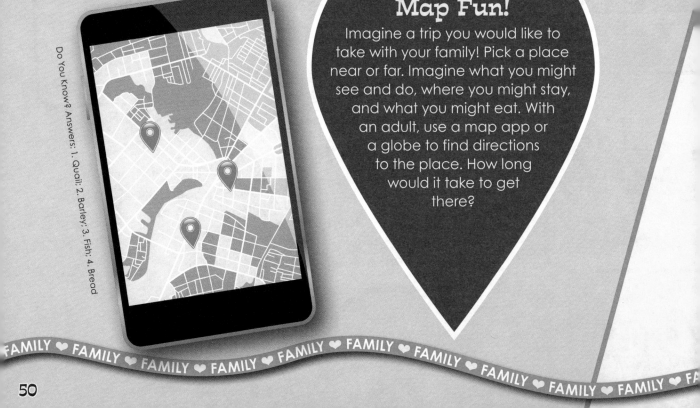

Make Time for Art Fun!

Celebrate God's love for your family with art. At the top of a piece of paper, write, "God loves . . ." and in the middle write the names of everyone in your family. Use markers, crayons, and stickers to decorate the paper, and hang it somewhere in your home where everyone can see it.

Do You Know?

Naomi, Ruth, and Orpah were suffering from a famine. They did not have enough food to eat. People in the Bible ate many different foods. Unscramble the words below to discover foods eaten in the Bible. Does your family like to eat these foods?

1. L Q U I A *(See Exodus 16:11-13.)*

◯ ◯ ◯ ◯ ◯

2. Y L B E R A *(See Ruth 2:17-18.)*

◯ ◯ ◯ ◯ ◯ ◯

3. I S F H *(See John 6:1-14.)*

◯ ◯ ◯ ◯

4. D B A R E *(See Matthew 26:26.)*

◯ ◯ ◯ ◯ ◯

51

David and Goliath

We trust God when we're scared.

The Israelites were trapped on a mountainside, facing an enemy army and its biggest, strongest man, Goliath. "Who will fight me?" roared Goliath. "I will do it," young David said. "God will protect me." David's smooth stone flew through the air. Down went Goliath. Up went the shout. **Hooray for David, who trusted God!**

Squiggles feels small. Goliath is so big!

How does YOUR face look when you feel small?

WHOM DO YOU TRUST?

WHO TRUSTS YOU?

Cut out this prayer and say it together. If you have a magnifying glass, use it to make the words even bigger.

HELP US to trust you, God, even when our fears are big. Amen.

David was small, but he trusted God to help him do a very big thing.
How do you know whom to trust?
Talk about the photos, and draw a picture of someone you trust.

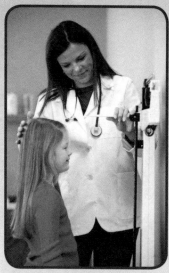

In the Bible AND In Our World!

David used a sling and a rock to defeat Goliath because it was a weapon he was very familiar with— shepherds such as David used them to protect sheep from predators. Today, and for thousands of years, shepherds also rely on special guard dogs to protect the sheep. These dogs are very alert and trustworthy.

Make Time for Decorating Fun!

Goliath used a fancy shield, but it didn't protect him against David. Make your own fancy shield out of a piece of cardboard or poster board. Decorate your shield with markers and other art materials. Write "God protects me" on your shield, and display it in your room. Ask an adult to read Ephesians 6:10-17 with you.

Do You Know?

When David volunteered to take on Goliath, he had to decide what he would take into battle with him. He considered all of the things below. Circle the items he decided to take into battle.

HELMET

SWORD

ARMOR

STONES AND SLING

BONUS QUESTION Why do you think David chose what he did?

_____

_____

Make Time for Game Fun!

David hit his target: Goliath's forehead. How is your aim? Practice by laying a hula hoop on the floor, stepping back several paces, and tossing small stuffed animals into the ring. Or go outside and toss a beanbag or ball through the hoop. Challenge yourself by moving farther from the target.

There's MORE to this story!

Read the WHOLE story in your Bible together! You can find it in a book named for the prophet Samuel:

1 Samuel 17:4-11, 32-50

In the Spark Story Bible, look for David and Goliath on pages 130-135.

Philistine is pronounced **fil-IS-teen**.

David said, "The LORD who rescued me from the **paw** of the **lion** and the **paw** of the **bear** will rescue me from the hand of this Philistine." Saul said to David, "Go, and the LORD be with you!"

1 Samuel 17:37

Add sound effects and action as you say this verse together.

When you say the word *lion*, roar like a lion and swat your **paws.**

Do the same at the word *bear.*

As you read the last sentence, stand at attention like a soldier.

Do You Know? Answer: David took the stones and sling into battle. Bonus Answer: The helmet, armor, and sword were difficult for David to use. They were heavy and awkward, and he was a young boy. The stones and sling were things he used every day to protect his sheep from predators such as wolves. David used what he was good at instead of trying to be someone he wasn't!

Jonah and the Big Fish

God gives us second chances.

God needed Jonah's help in Nineveh, but Jonah ran away. He took a boat in the other direction and ended up in the sea. Gulp! Jonah was swallowed by a gigantic, stinky, smelly fish. He prayed for God to forgive him. Finally, the fish spit him out. Jonah went to Nineveh and told the people to live the way God wants. **The people of Nineveh believed him and changed!**

Squiggles feels sorry. He wants to try again. How does YOUR face look when you feel sorry?

LOVING, listening God, thank you for second chances every day. Amen.

Cut out this prayer and place it under a pillow. Are there things you wish you could do over tomorrow? Share ideas with your family, and say the prayer together at bedtime.

WHAT JOBS DO YOU AVOID?

HOW DO YOU SHOW YOU'RE SORRY?

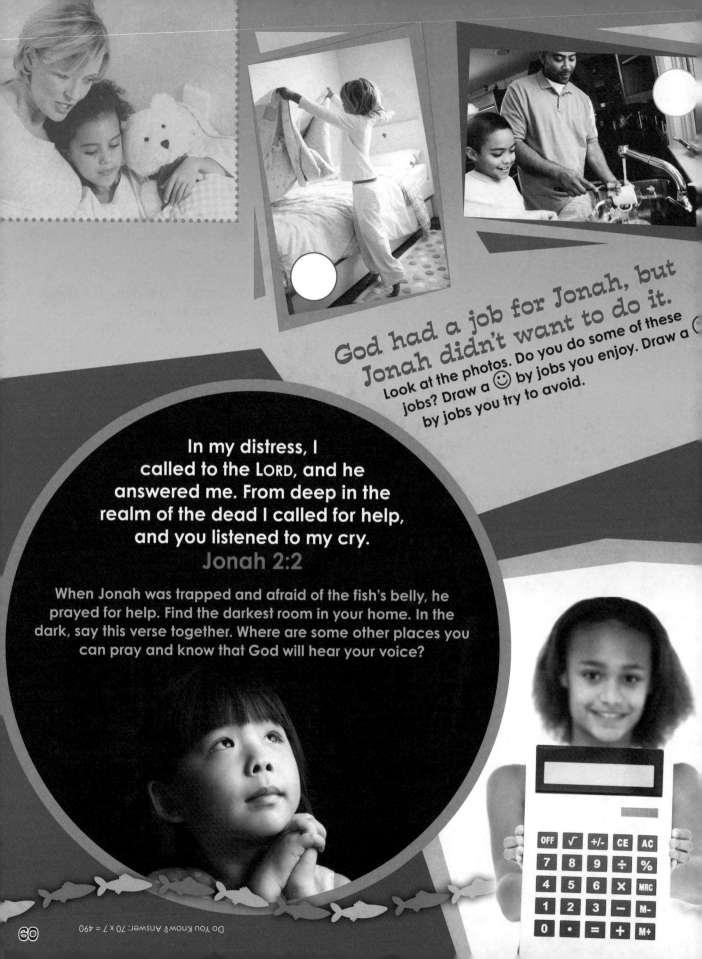

God had a job for Jonah, but Jonah didn't want to do it.

Look at the photos. Do you do some of these jobs? Draw a ☺ by jobs you enjoy. Draw a ☹ by jobs you try to avoid.

In my distress, I called to the LORD, and he answered me. From deep in the realm of the dead I called for help, and you listened to my cry.

Jonah 2:2

When Jonah was trapped and afraid of the fish's belly, he prayed for help. Find the darkest room in your home. In the dark, say this verse together. Where are some other places you can pray and know that God will hear your voice?

There's MORE to this story!

Read the WHOLE story in your Bible together! You can find it in the book named for the prophet in this story:

Jonah 1–4

In the Spark Story Bible, look for *Jonah and the Big Fish* on pages 180-183.

Make Time for More Fun!

Play a "Jonah and the fish" tag game the next time you're at a pool or playing in water. One person can be the big fish and everyone else can be Jonah. How does it feel to run away in the water? How do you think Jonah felt when he was running away from God?

Do You Know?

God gave second chances to Jonah and the people of Nineveh. But God doesn't stop at two chances!

In Matthew 18:21-22, the disciple Peter asks Jesus how many times we should forgive. Some versions of the Bible say 70 times. Other versions say 70 times 7. How many times would that be?

$70 \times 7 =$ _____

That's a lot of forgiveness!

Fiery Furnace

We can always trust God.

Squiggles feels
afraid. The
furnace is
hot.

How does
YOUR face
look when you
feel afraid?

King Nebuchadnezzar was mad! Shadrach, Meshach, and Abednego worshiped only God and refused to bow down to the king's huge gold statue. The king ordered the men to be thrown into a hot furnace. It was scary, but God sent an angel to protect them. The king was amazed and knew that God was with them.

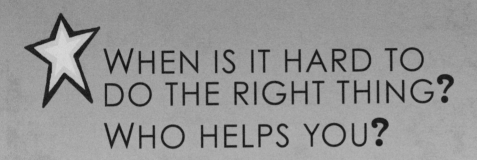

WHEN IS IT HARD TO DO THE RIGHT THING? WHO HELPS YOU?

Cut out this prayer and place it on a table. Have an adult put a lighted or electric candle on the table. Look at the flame and say the prayer together.

GOD, sometimes it is hard to do the right thing. Help us to trust you. Amen.

The three friends trusted God, and God protected them in the fiery furnace.

Fire and heat are helpful, but also dangerous! God gives us people and tools to protect us. Match the hot photos with the person or thing that helps protect us.

There's MORE to this story!

Read the WHOLE story in your Bible together! You can find it in the prophets section of the Old Testament:

Daniel 3:19-30

In the Spark Story Bible, look for Fiery Furnace on pages 170-173.

DELIVER US FROM EVIL . . . AND DELIVER US FROM EVIL . . . AND DELIVER US FROM EVIL . . . AND DELIVER US F

Then Nebuchadnezzar said,

"Praise be to the God of Shadrach, Meshach, and Abednego, who has sent his angel and rescued his servants."

Daniel 3:28a

Play a simple trust game. In an open space, set up a "fiery furnace" by scattering small stuffed toys as "flames." In pairs, one person uses words to guide another person, whose eyes are closed, through the furnace without touching a flame. Start each round by saying the verse together.

Make Time for More Fun

Make a fiery furnace snack. Put graham crackers on a cookie sheet. Sprinkle chocolate chips and mini marshmallows on each cracker. Put three bear-shaped graham crackers on top. Pop them in the "fiery furnace" (375°F or 190°C oven) for 5 minutes. The chocolate and marshmallows melt but the bears are fine! Let your snack cool before eating. Talk about safety in your kitchen.

Do You Know?

Shadrach, Meshach, and Abednego were forced to work for King Nebuchadnezzar. They tried to do the right thing and trust God that they would be okay. It wasn't easy, but God was with them. **Practice saying the names of the people and places in this story:**

Abednego is pronounced **uh-BEHD-nee-go.**

Shadrach is pronounced **SHAY-drak.**

Meshach is pronounced **MEE-shak.**

Babylon is pronounced **BAB-ih-luhn.**

Nebuchadnezzar is pronounced **neh-byou-kuhd-NEHZ-er.**

Tip: If you need help, go on the Internet with an adult and search "Bible pronunciation" to find audio files that provide the pronunciation of these names.

... AND DELIVER US FROM EVIL ... AND DELIVER US FROM EVIL

Daniel and the

We can ask God for help.

Daniel worshiped God. But the law said that everyone had to worship King Darius. Thump! Daniel was thrown in a pit of snarling lions. Daniel prayed, and the lions closed their toothy grins and rested their heads on their paws. In the morning, Daniel was still alive. King Darius was surprised! **From that day, King Darius believed in God.**

Lions

⭐ WHEN DO YOU PRAY FOR HELP?
HOW DOES GOD HELP YOU?

Squiggles feels afraid. The lions are growling!

How does **YOUR** face look
when you feel afraid?

Cut out this prayer and slip it into a
backpack or tote. Read the prayer with
your family before you leave for the day
and when you get home.

**ALL day long,
wherever we go,
God is with us,
God's help
shows. Amen.**

Sometimes we are afraid like Daniel.

Sometimes we are surprised like King Darius. God is with us no matter what.

Look at the photos and draw how your face would look if each one were happening to you. How is God with you when you feel like this?

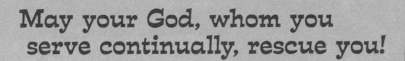

May your God, whom you serve continually, rescue you!

Daniel 6:16

King Darius knew that Daniel was faithful to God and prayed to God every day.

Say the Bible verse together. Then have one person read the verse, leaving out one word. Who can remember the missing word? Pass this page to another reader, who will leave out a different word.

There's **MORE** to this story!

Read the WHOLE story in your Bible together! You can find it in the prophets section of the Old Testament:

Daniel 6:1-28

In the Spark Story Bible, look for *Daniel and the Lions* on pages 174-179.

Make Time for Roaring Fun!

Roar like a lion! Who in your family can roar the loudest? When Daniel prayed in the lions' den, God shut the lions' mouths. Trying roaring with your mouth shut. Who can make the silliest closed-mouth roar?

Do You Know?

Many people in the Bible prayed to God for help when they were in trouble. This verse is from a poem in the Bible that was written to remind us that God will always help us. Finish the verse by unscrambling the words below.

God is our refuge and

☐☐☐☐☐☐☐☐

an ever present

☐☐☐ in

☐☐☐☐☐☐☐ .

Psalm 46:1

TENGHTSR

EPLH

BRLEOTU

THFUL

COLOR THIS WORD. To be *faithful* means to have a strong belief in and to always be true to someone or something. Daniel was faithful to God when he prayed only to God and not to the king, and when he trusted that God would help him. God was faithful to Daniel by protecting him in the lions' den.

Make Time for Praying Fun!

Who in your community needs help? Look through a worship bulletin for prayer requests, skim your local newspaper to find stories about people in need, and think of friends who need help. Make a list of their names and say a prayer for them.

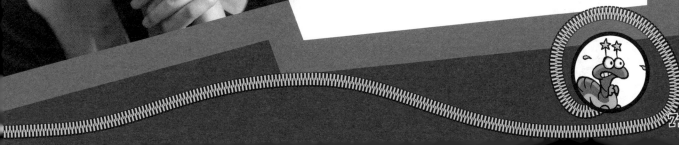

71

Queen Esther

Let's do the right thing!

Esther was a beautiful Jewish woman who became queen. Before she lived in the palace she lived with her cousin Mordecai. A man who worked for the king, Haman, made some bad rules. Mordecai refused to follow them. This made Haman angry. He threatened to have all the Jews killed! Queen Esther was afraid the king would be mad if she told him about Haman's plans. **But she did the right thing, and the Jewish people were saved!**

Haman is pronounced **HAY-mun.**

Squiggles feels afraid. Haman has bad plans.

How does **YOUR** face look when you feel afraid?

WHO HELPS YOU WHEN YOU'RE AFRAID?

WHAT HELPS YOU BE BRAVE?

Mordecai is pronounced **MORE-deh-keye.**

Cut out this prayer and say it together. Then cut it into strips (see reverse side), roll one strip around a finger, and tape it together, like a ring. Wear it to remind you to do the right thing!

MIGHTY GOD, give us the courage of Queen Esther when we have to do scary things. Amen.

73

Queen Esther did the right thing, even though it was scary.

Look at the photos. Rate how easy or hard each of these things is to do by writing a number between 1 and 4 on each photo.

1 = Very easy
2 = Easy
3 = Hard
4 = Very hard

Purim gift basket

Purim is pronounced **POO-rim.**

In the Bible AND In Our World!

After Queen Esther warned the king of Haman's evil plans, the Jewish people celebrated. The celebration is called **Purim**, and Jewish people still celebrate it today. Purim traditions include reading from the book of Esther, giving gifts of food to friends, giving food to the poor, and eating a festive meal.

Make Time for Drama Fun!

One of the ways Jewish people celebrate the festival of Purim is to act out the story of Queen Esther. Get some of your family and friends together, and as you read the story in your Bible, act it out. Whenever the reader says the name *Haman*, everybody should respond with a loud and dramatic "Booo!" When the reader says the names *Mordecai* or *Esther*, everyone should cheer as loud as they can.

Do You Know?

There are many stories in the Bible of God working through women like Esther. Draw a line from the picture of the woman to the description of what she did.

1. Deborah
(see Judges 4:4)

A. She prayed for a son who would serve God.

2. Ruth
(see Ruth 1:16-17)

B. She was loyal to her mother-in-law, Naomi.

3. Hannah
(see 1 Samuel 1:9-11)

C. She was a wise and brave judge who delivered the Israelites from enemies.

There's MORE to this story!

Read the WHOLE story in your Bible together! You can find it in the book named for Queen Esther:

Esther 2:5-18; 3:1-6; 8:1-17

In the Spark Story Bible, look for Queen Esther on pages 152-157.

Esther again pleaded with the king, falling at his feet and weeping. She begged him to put an end to the evil plan of Haman the Agagite, which he had devised against the Jews.

Esther 8:3

God worked through Esther to help keep God's people safe. Read this verse together. What did Esther do to keep people safe? What can you do to help keep people and God's creation safe? Talk about it!

Make Time for Baking Fun!

Hamantaschen cookies, also known as "Haman's pockets," are a traditional treat when celebrating Purim. These triangular-shaped cookies are usually baked with poppy seed, prune, or apricot fillings. With an adult, find a recipe on the Internet by searching for "Hamantaschen recipe." After the cookies have baked and cooled, share the cookies and the story of Queen Esther with friends.

A Note for Grown-Ups

At Sparkhouse Family, we believe faith formation isn't something that only happens when kids are in church or hearing a Bible story in Sunday school. It's an ongoing process that's part of every moment of a child's life. Each interaction with a caring adult shows kids what love looks like. Each playful interaction with a friend taps into their God-given joy and delight. Moments of daydreaming and imaginative play develop their ability to see God in the world.

We also know that many families want to create intentional times of spiritual formation for their kids. That's where the Spark Story Bible Play and Learn books come in. Whether you've already introduced your children to the Bible or are just starting to talk about it, these books make a great resource for helping your family dive into God's Word. They offer a hands-on approach to teaching Bible stories that will resonate with your whole family. Together, you'll explore these stories through games, puzzles, conversation, prayer, and easy-to-manage activities. You can spend ten minutes on a story or a whole afternoon—it's all up to you.

And you won't need a long list of supplies to get started—some crayons, a pair of scissors, and a few items you can find around your house. So make a little time, grab a handful of crayons, and create fun, meaningful family time with God.

Thanks!

Sparkhouse Family

Image Credits

Image Credits (continued)